TIMEOUT

FOR

TEACHERS

Over 150 PRAYERS FOR TEACHERS to develop a spiritual relationship with God.

CHRISTIE SOLOMON CAREATHERS

CHRISTIAN CONCEPTS

CC

Scripture quotations, unless otherwise indicated, are taken from *The New Oxford Annotated Bible*, authorized New Revised Standard Version.

Timeout For Teachers
Copyright © 2004
by Christie Solomon Careathers

ISBN 0-9719200-0-1

All rights reserved. No part of this publication may be reproduced or transmitted in any form or by any means-electronic, mechanical, photocopy, recording, or any other-except for brief quotations in printed reviews, without written permission of the publisher.

Published by
Christian Concepts
16773 Edinborough
Detroit, MI 48219-4019

Printed in the United States by Morris Publishing
3212 East Highway 30
Kearney, NE 68847
1-800-650-7888

TEACHER:

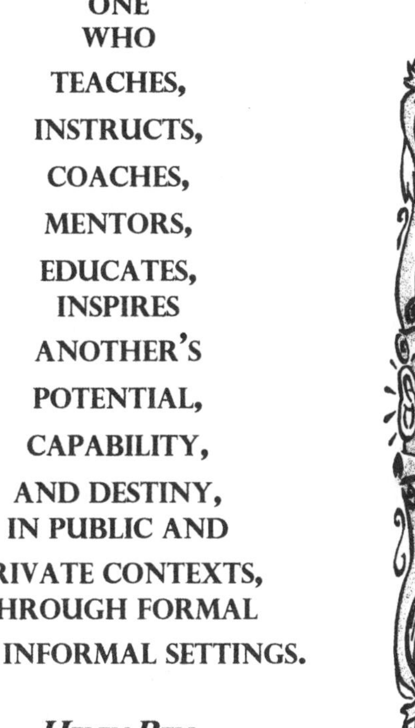

ONE
WHO
TEACHES,
INSTRUCTS,
COACHES,
MENTORS,
EDUCATES,
INSPIRES
ANOTHER'S
POTENTIAL,
CAPABILITY,
AND DESTINY,
IN PUBLIC AND
PRIVATE CONTEXTS,
THROUGH FORMAL
AND INFORMAL SETTINGS.

HELEN BELL
MARIO CALHOUN
BRONTE' DINKINS
PATTI BURNETTE JONES
VERONA MORTON
JAMES ROSS
DR. JACQUELINE TILLES

Contents

INTRODUCTION 5

I. ATTITUDE ......BEHAVIOR 11
College Student Profile

II. LOVE.....COMPASSION 37
Middle School Student Profile

III. MORALS.........VALUES 62
High School Student Profile

IV. FUTURE.......PROMISES 88
Elementary School Student Profile

V. GUIDANCE.......CHOICES 114
High School Student Profile

VI. TEACHABLE SPIRITS 140
Middle School Student Profile

VII. WISDOM......KNOWLEDGE 166
University Student Profile

VIII. TRUST IN GOD 198
Private School Student Profile

Introduction

There are several hopes for educators as they engage in *Timeout for Teachers*. First and foremost, this is a book on Spirituality involving reading prayers, reflection and responses. Spirituality is defined as your consciousness and your connection to God. This book is designed for teachers, instructors, lecturers, faculty, college professors, coaches and Christian educators to use in fostering a deeper relationship through a purposeful timeout period of prayer.

Secondly, it is my desire for you as educators to embrace the "teaching field" as a specific and Divine calling rather than view your instructional efforts as work or as an underpaid and unappreciated career choice. It was not until 1982 after ten years of teaching that the connection was made for me. I thought I had been doing something noble and admirable by teaching English to inner city teens. Of course, now I am eternally grateful for the guidance of the Holy Spirit who revealed to me that teaching was not a job or career, but a ministry unto God.

When *Timeout for Teachers* is used as your own spiritual formational tool, you will feel free to delve into the inner core of your heart and subscribe to your primary charge by God to teach students. Therefore, personal and regular periods of devotion are the secret to making this guidebook relevant and formative for you as you prepare for interaction and instruction. It is my belief that your spiritual development is directly reflected in your student's success. Your insight respecting the power and presence of God can be evidenced in how you implement your teaching strategies. As a result, each chapter of *Timeout for Teachers* contains the following components:

- 8 Different chapter topics
- Read section: Twenty or more Scriptures from Old or New Testament relative to chapter topic
- Reflect section: Narrative of student
- Blank Respond page for your response to chapter experience

Take notice that I've included two fundamental practices commonly adopted to get the most out of prayer and Scriptures. Today's prominent scholars use both the *Ignatian* Method of meditating on Scriptures, and the *Lectio Divinia* Method of praying the Scriptures.

THE IGNATIAN METHOD

The reflection narratives included in *Timeout for Teachers* are shared for your camaraderie in the teaching ministry as you see yourself in the unfolding drama of the redemption and formation of your student. After reading the narratives for each chapter, you should ask yourself, "what does this say to me?" How are my student's experiences similar to these? What did the teachers of these students do to minister to their concerns? How can I as an educator address the life issues of my own students? How can I make a difference? What can I do to let my hurting students know that God cares for them?

LECTIO DIVINA
(Praying the Scriptures)

Praying the Scripture is the practice of allowing the words of the Bible to literally form your prayer. This method has been used for centuries as a way to stay spiritually linked to God. Each chapter in *Timeout for Teachers* has over 20 Scriptures related to the chapter title. It is full of opportunities to engage the Word of God through prayer. Together there are over 150 Scriptures that you may use as creatively as needful.

Timeout for Teachers is a deliberate effort on your part to arrange time during your day to speak to God. In other words, you will be engaging in intercessory prayer for your students on a daily, weekly or monthly basis. Your frequency directs your faith. Your faith directs your focus. Your focus frames your spirituality. It is this purposeful "*timeout with God*" that you seek.

During your prayer timeout periods, lay aside your classroom troubles, cares and fears. Spend time reading, reflecting and responding to the Word of God contained in each chapter. Get to know God, his heart, his words, his voice and his power. Know that the "effectual fervent prayers of the righteous avails much."

This book is not designed sequentially but rather circumstantially. You are encouraged to receive optimal benefits by completing the read, reflect and respond portions. I further invite you to complete an entire chapter before proceeding to another. However, if God so directs, then feel free to select your own path according to your desired embarking point. Although I have not specified a rigid time period or frequency rate, with the guidance of the Holy Spirit you may consider praying for several students concurrently or one student for a pre-set interval. For example, 'Teacher A' may pray a specific Scripture for two weeks on behalf of one student, while 'Teacher B' might pray every Scripture in a chapter inserting a different name from their roster, for a whole month. It is your relationship with God that directs your concerns and prayers for them.

However, it is anticipated the teacher will reach a "centering moment", so overcome the guilt often accompanied with feelings of inadequacies as a teacher. Remember that you have been called by God and for that reason consider the following tips:

- Set aside a minimum of fifteen minutes in regular practice to engage yourself in prayer as an educator. This optimal timeout with God could be initiated immediately before your duties. It's quality time that you pursue.
- As you read God's Holy Word, meditate until your mind and spirit are quiet. Do not think of the things of the world, the flesh or the enemy. Decide to think God's thoughts. Find a private place with God. Get into your own corner. This may be at home, in the classroom before students arrive or anywhere that you may be alone with God.
- Pray the promises of the Scripture as related to your student's specific situation.
- Insert your student's names into the printed scriptural prayer, and pray sincerely and confidently that God hears your prayers.
- When your reading, reflection and respond period is completed, experience rest, relaxation, refreshing and renewal, as you have received a Word from the Lord Jesus Christ.

- Keep a daily journal to record the experiences that you have so they can be referenced in the future as "spiritual renewal in the classroom."

Remember that you are a vital and most significant member in the larger scheme of life. You are responsible for impacting hundreds and thousands of students, young and old, male and female. God has given you a tremendous trustworthiness and you must know that everyone is not gifted in this manner. Be careful to take this charge as somberly and humbly as possible. I encourage you to pray, pray, pray and then pray again for your students. Their body, soul and spirit need nurturing, guiding and guarding and for a short period of the day, you are given that charge.

If in fact you are called to teach, instruct, mentor or direct another, then you must approach each and every opportunity with your student's future destiny in mind. It becomes imperative that you take time to prepare yourself for a mighty work.

As a final thought, I am reminded of God's purpose for us his creations. "*I know the thoughts that I think towards you, thoughts of good and not of evil to your expected end.*" (Jeremiah 29:11)

CHAPTER ONE

ATTITUDES~BEHAVIOR

Read Prayers of Intercession

1

NEW ATTITUDE

Show

____

how to put off
her old self,
which is being corrupted
by its deceitful desires,
and make her new in
the attitude of her mind.
Cause her to put off
falsehood and speak truthfully,
and to refrain from sin
when she is angry.
Above all,
do not let ________
do anything
that would give
the devil a foothold in her life.
Ephesians 4:22-27

2

PAST HISTORY CONFESSION

Let

____

be quick to confess sin,
knowing that you
are faithful and just,
and that you will
forgive him his sins
and purify him
from all unrighteousness.
Don't let him
get bogged down
by his past mistakes;
rather, remind him that
he is a new creation in Christ,
that the old has gone
and the new has come.
1 John 1:9

3

JEALOUS

O Lord,
do not let

____

become jealous
like Miriam.
Do not
punish her
for her sin
she so foolishly
committed.
O God,
please heal her.
Numbers 12:11-13

4

BAD ADVICE

Let

____________________,

be as a happy youth,
who does not follow
the advice of the wicked
or take the path
that sinners tread,
or sit in the seat of scoffers.
Take delight in your law,
and let her meditate
on it day and night,
so that whatever
she does
will prosper.
Psalm 1:1-3

5

ASSOCIATION

Keep men
of perverse heart
far from

_________________________,

and let
her have
nothing
to do
with evil.
Psalm 101:4

6

Perfect Example

Thank you
for showing
compassion to us.
I pray that

____

would follow
your example,
being compassionate
and gracious,
slow to anger,
and abounding
in love.
Psalm 103:8

7

Gossip

Don't let

____

exclude her peers
or participate
in gossip,
since a
perverse person
stirs up
dissension,
and a gossip
separates
close friends.
Proverbs 16:28

8

Generosity

Let

____

open
his arms
to the poor
and extend
his hands
to the needy.
Proverbs 31:20

9

FORGIVENESS

Let

---

develop
the spirit
of forgiveness,
not seven times,
but seventy-seven times-
and more.
Matthew 18:22

10

Bless Enemies

Cause

____

to love her enemies,
to do good
to those
who hate her,
to bless those
who curse her,
to pray for those
who mistreat her.
Help

____

do to others
as she would have
them do to her.
Luke 6:27-31

11

SALVATION

Cause

---

to confess
with his lips
that Jesus is Lord,
and that
he would believe
in his heart
that Christ
has been raised
from the dead.
so that
he can be saved.
Romans 10:9

12

DO HER PART

Let

____

use her gifts
for the common good,
recognizing how she fits
into the body of Christ
and using her special abilities
to build up
and complement others.
1 Corinthians 12:7-26

13

Harmony

Let

____

live in harmony
with her classmates,
being sympathetic,
compassionate,
and humble.
Don't let

____

repay evil with evil
or insult with insult,
but with blessing.
1 Peter 3:8-9

14

Kindness

Let

____

be kind
and compassionate
to others,
forgiving them
just as in Christ
God forgave him.
Ephesians 4:32

15

Christ-Like

Show

____

that whatever he does,
in word or deed,
he should do
everything
in the name
of the Lord Jesus,
giving thanks
to God the Father
through Jesus Christ.
Colossians 3:17

16

Obedience

Let

____

understand
your word says
that children
should obey
their parents
in everything,
for this is
your acceptable
duty
in the Lord.
Colossians 3:20

17

RESPECT

Cause

---

to be wise
in the way he acts
toward his teachers,
making the most
of every opportunity.
Let his conversation
be always full of grace,
seasoned with salt,
so that he will know
how to respectfully
and graciously answer
his teachers' questions.
Colossians 4:5-6

18

Hospitality

Do not let

____

forget to
entertain strangers,
for by doing so
some people have
entertained angels
without knowing it.
Prompt her to remember
those in prison
as if she were
their fellow prisoner,
and those who are mistreated
as if she herself
were suffering.
Hebrews 13:2-3

19

POWER

Do not give

---

a spirit of cowardice,
but rather
a spirit of power
and of love
and of self-discipline.
2 Timothy 1:7

20

Argumentative

Do not permit

____

to be quarrelsome;
instead, cause him to be gentle,
patient, and humble,
especially when others
in the classroom
are in the wrong...
because then they
will be more likely,
with God's help,
to turn away
from their wrong ideas
and believe
what is true.
2 Timothy 2:24-26

Timeout Reflections on Jason

College Student Profile

REFLECT ON JASON

Jason was only in his second semester of community college. His parents insisted that he enroll right after high school. He managed to complete the first semester two classes with a low 'C' grade in Math 105 and a 'D' grade in English 108. He felt a little disappointed in his grade for Math, but he was extremely surprised and needless to say delighted to see the grade for his beginning English course. So this semester he felt a little comfortable to register for the next level English course. Jason had figured this community college thing out.

Fortunately for him, he worked the day shift. This allowed him a brief run to the house, shower, change and arrive to class only fifteen minutes late, if he didn't stop to eat, if he timed the lights just right, or if he didn't make plans with the fellows.

Jason hadn't really made up his mind yet to be a student or a college Casanova. His plan this term was to meet a few female classmates and exchange numbers, in case he missed class, which he definitely planned to do. Jason seemed to be working his female classmates just right and he hoped something more might develop with one of them. She seemed interested in more than English discussions. He noticed that she always volunteered to partner with him in the group discussions.

However, during the third week of class, the instructor started calling on the students individually to respond to the literary assignment.

Jason was never prepared. He hadn't read any of the narratives. He hadn't turned in one paper. He gave excuse after excuse. When the instructor gave out the monthly evaluation forms, Jason's performance was less than adequate. After the second evaluation, Jason became argumentative, defensive and noticeably more absent.

Respond

CHAPTER TWO
LOVE~COMPASSION

READ PRAYERS OF INTERCESSION

21

EVIL DESIRES

Let

____

flee the evil desires
of youth
and pursue
righteousness,
faith,
love,
and peace,
and let him enjoy
the companionship
of those
who call on you
out of a
pure heart.
2 Timothy 2:22

22

Peaceful Sleep

Let the light
of your face
shine upon
______________.

Fill his heart
with joy,
and let him
lie down
and sleep in peace.
Psalm 4:6

23

Pleasant Classroom

Make our classroom
a good and
pleasant place,
where both male
and female
work together
in unity.
Psalm 133:1

24

Wonderfully Made

Show

____

that she is
fearfully and wonderfully made,
and that
your works are wonderful.
Teach her
that she is precious
in your sight,
and that you love her.
Psalm 139:14

25

MORAL CONVERSATION

Set a guard over
_______________________’s

mouth,
O Lord;
keep watch over her lips.
Don’t let her heart
be drawn to what is evil
or allow her
to take part
in wicked deeds.
Psalm 141:3-4

26

Diligence

Let

____

be diligent,
O Lord,
and satisfy
all his desires.
Proverbs 13:4

27

GODLY LOVE

Teach

__________________________,

your word that says,
I will not
leave you orphaned.
to know your commands
and obey them,
thereby demonstrating
his love for you.
Let him know
your promised reward:
that "he who loves me
will be loved by my Father,
and I too will love him
and show myself to him."
Love him, and show yourself to him, Lord.
John 14:18-21

28

GOD'S FRIENDSHIP

Count

____

as one of your friends,
Lord. Let him live
according to your words
in John 15:12-14,
loving others
as you have loved him...
obeying your commands...
and finding his security
in the reality
of your life-giving love.

29

Conquerors

Do not let
anything separate

____

from your love.
When trouble, hardship,
persecution, danger,
or any need arises,
let

____

remember
that we are
"more than conquerors"
and that nothing
can separate him
from the love of God
that is in
Christ Jesus our Lord.
Romans 8:35-39

30

GOOD PLANS

Let

____

be glad for
all you are
planning for her.
Thank you for loving

____

Let her learn
to be patient
in trouble,
and prayerful always.
Romans 12:12

31

COMFORT

Comfort

____

in all her troubles,
so that she may
comfort those in any trouble
with the comfort received
from you,
precious Lord.
2 Corinthians 1:4

32

Gentleness

Make

____

and her teachers
completely humble and gentle.
Let them be patient,
bearing with
one another in love.
Ephesians 4:2

33

Wholesome Conversation

Do not let any
unwholesome talk
come out of

____

mouth,
but only what is helpful
for building others up
according to their needs,
that it may benefit
those who listen.
Ephesians 4:29

34

Discernment

This is my prayer:
that
____________________'s

love may abound
more and more
in knowledge
and depth of insight,
so that she may
be able to discern
what is best
and may be pure and blameless
until the day of Christ,
filled with the
fruit of righteousness
that comes
through Jesus Christ.
Philippians 1:9-11

35

ANXIETY

As we pray for

________________,

do not let us
be anxious about anything,
but in everything,
by prayer and petition,
with thanksgiving,
let us always
remember to present
our requests to you.
And let your peace, which
transcends all understanding,
guard our hearts
and our minds
in Christ Jesus.
Philippians 4:6-7

36

Lure of Money

Keep

__________________'s

life free from
the love of money
and let him be content
with what he has,
knowing that you,
O Lord will never leave him
or forsake him.
Let him be like Paul
who knew how to be content
in any and every situation
whether well fed or hungry,
whether living in plenty
or in want.
Hebrews 13:5

37

JOY

Let

____

be filled with the joy
given by the Holy Spirit.
Let

____

be joyful always,
pray continually,
and give thanks
in all circumstances,
for this
is your will
for him
in Christ Jesus.
1 Thessalonians 1:6; 5:16-18

38

Physical Healing

Thank you for
loving

____

Jesus,
and for bearing

____________________'s

sins in your body
on the tree,
and that by your wounds

____

is healed.
1 Peter 2:24

39

SHARING

Your word says
that if anyone
has material possessions
and sees his brother
in need but has
no pity on him,
how can the love of God
be in him?
Therefore, let

____

not love with mere words,
but let him love others
with actions
and in truth.
1 John 3:17-18

40

HARMONY

Let

____

live in harmony
with her classmates,
being sympathetic,
compassionate,
and humble.
Don't let

____

repay evil with evil
or insult with insult,
but with blessing.
1 Peter 3:8-9

Timeout Reflections on Crystal

Middle School Student Profile

REFLECT ON CRYSTAL

Crystal was tall for her age. In the seventh grade she towered all female teachers and even a couple of her male teachers. Knowing that she usually received her handful of attention, Crystal started slacking off in her studies. But it wasn't because she couldn't grasp the concepts, she was brilliant.

Crystal came from a single parent home where her mother and aunt lived together. Her life provided little to no interaction with her father. The void was evident and her search to fill the emptiness started way too early for her own good. As it turned out, Crystal struggled with her lanky somewhat less than overt feminine characteristics and ventured into promiscuity.

Her interests surfaced without much parental interruption, because her mother worked long hours. Crystal was left to grow up fast and relatively alone. Her survival skills developed out of an attempt to portray herself older because she didn't fit in with her own age group. This curiosity was enhanced due to a constant pursuit by high school boys and even adult men.

Crystal admitted that it went too far when she invited a cute stranger home while her mother was at work. Everyday, she giggled at his cat calls and car horn blowing as she walked home from school. That day things went so terribly wrong. Fortunately, God was there.

Chapter Three
Morals~Values

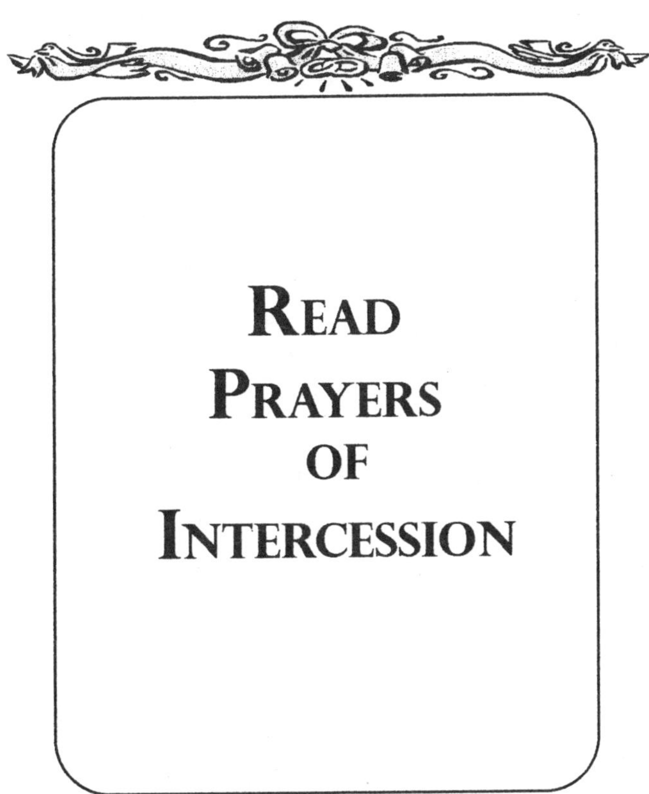

Read Prayers of Intercession

41

Made in your Image

Let

____

appreciate that
he is made in your image,
according to your likeness,
and with a standard of excellency.
Let him know that
he was given
dominion over
the fish of the sea,
and over
the birds of the air,
and over every creeping thing
that creeps upon the earth.
Genesis 1:26

42

Integrity

Let

____

learn to model
himself after men
who display good works.
In all respects of life,
let him show
integrity and gravity.
Titus 2:7

43

DISCIPLINE

Clarify for

____

how discipline
always seems painful for her
rather than pleasant
at the time,
but later it yields
the peaceful fruit of righteousness
to those who have been
trained by it.
Hebrews 12:11

44

HOLY BODY

Let

____

avoid fornication.
Reveal to him
that his body
is a temple
of the Holy Spirit,
residing within him.
Reveal to him
that he is not his own
but brought with a price
to glorify you
with his body.
1 Corinthians 6:18-20

45

TRUTH

Let

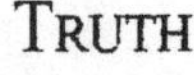

learn to know
and use truth,
so that the truth
will make him free.
John 8:32

46

Respect

Allow

____

to develop respect
for you.
For fear is the
beginning of wisdom,
and knowledge
of the Holy One is insight.
Proverbs 9:10

47

Good Character

Permit
____________________’s

light to shine before us,
so that we may see
his good works
and give glory to you,
our Father
in heaven.
Matthew 5:16

48

SPECIAL GIFT

Make clear to

____

how she has gifts
that differ
according to the
grace you
have given to us.
Whether her gifts
be in exhortation,
generosity,
diligence,
or cheerfulness.
Romans 12:6-8

49

Honorable

Grant that

____

will love her classmates
with mutual affection.
Cause opportunities
for her to outdo
the other students
by showing them honor.
Romans 12:10

50

Living Sacrifice Body

Sanction

---

to present her body
as a living sacrifice,
holy and acceptable
to you God.
This is her chance
to engage in
spiritual worship.
Romans 12:1

51

Cheerful Giver

Teach

---

that the one who
sows sparingly
will also reap sparingly
and the one who
sows bountifully,
will also
reap bountifully.
Help her make up her mind
not reluctantly
or under compulsion,
for you O' God
love a cheerful giver.
2 Corinthians 9:6-7

52

Purposeful Actions

Make

---

recognize it is you God
who is at work
in his life
enabling him to will
and work for
your good pleasure.
Philippians 2:13

53

FRUIT OF THE SPIRIT

Share with

____

that he is
one of your
chosen ones.
Clothe him with
compassion,
kindness,
humility,
meekness,
and patience.
Colossians 3:12

54

CORRECTION

Make clear to

____

that you, Oh God
will discipline those
whom you love
and that you
will chastise every one
whom you call yours.
Hebrews 12:6

55

Discipline

Thank you
for disciplining
____________________,

and for preparing him
to share in your holiness.
Use this discipline process-
however painful
to train him
and produce a harvest
of righteousness
and peace
in his life.
Hebrews 12:10-11

56

SELF-CONTROL

Help

____

demonstrate a life
of self-control .
Help him refrain
from developing
a quick temper,
a quick mouth,
and quick actions.
Titus 2:6

57

AUTHORITY

I pray that

____

would display honor
and respect to
everyone in authority
over her.
Encourage her
to love the
family of believers,
and to fear God.
1 Peter 2: 17

58

RESPECT FOR ELDERS

Let

____

come to know
that as he
is the younger
he must accept
the authority
of the elders.
1 Peter 5:5

59

SPIRIT FILLED

Fill

with your Holy Spirit,
that she might bear
the Spirit's fruit;
love, joy, peace.
patience, kindness,
goodness, faithfulness,
gentleness,
and self-control.
Galatians 5:22-23

60

STRUCTURE

Help

---

structure himself
and stay alert,
for his adversary the devil
is like a roaring lion
prowling around
looking for
him to devour.
1 Peter 5:6-8

Timeout Reflections On Fatima

High School Student Profile

REFLECT ON FATIMA

Fatima was a beautiful teenage girl of Arabic descent. She had been in America since she was five years old. In fact, she held a dual citizenship. Her father wanted his younger children to go to an American School. He allowed her to attend a public high school, even though most females from their country did not attend school past the eighth grade. It was just their way. Her mother married her father at the age of fourteen back home and started having children right away.

However, that was the limit of her father's progressiveness. Fatima was not allowed to date and she had to keep her hair covered in public. She was not even allowed to be in the company of males even while at school. Yet she caught the eye of an American male student, and he caught hers.

During her senior year, Fatima became noticeably immersed in American customs and traditions. Fatima attended the Homecoming Pep Rally and mingled amongst her classmates without as much reserve and etiquette as she normally displayed.

At the Christmas holiday celebration, she accepted a Christmas present and kept it in her locker the entire school year. At

Valentines' Day she carried a teddy bear and balloon throughout the day. At day's end she also placed it in her locker. Frequently, Fatima was spotted hurriedly exiting from the back hallway. The hallway that housed no classrooms. Sometimes the American male student would appear before her and at other times, her male friend would cautiously appear a careful few seconds later. Fatima started experimenting with a real high school crush.

Rumors started floating around the school and attitudes developed. What might have otherwise been considered teenage behavior turned into tension and a cultural divide. In fact, the whole year almost seemed like a mini "Westside Story" drama, with fight and all.

In the spring, Fatima was absent from school for a few weeks. Her teachers and the school officials received no indication that Fatima was sick. After about a month, Fatima returned back to school without explanation. Her demeanor seemed more subdued and she arrived and departed school daily by a ride from either her father or her older brother.

At the end of the school term, she graduated and boarded a plane the next day back to her home country.

RESPOND

Chapter Four

Future~Promises

Read Prayers of Intercession

61

Promise

Help

to know that
your hand is
not to short to save
and that your ear is
not too dull to hear him
when he calls out to you.
Isaiah 59:1

62

Assurance

Show

---

that no weapon
fashioned against her
shall prosper,
and that she should
confute every tongue
that rises against
her in judgement.
Isaiah 54:17

63

Vows

Teach

____

that what
he has vowed
he must pay.
Jonah 2:9

64

Day of Trouble

Show

____

that you are good
and that you will be
a stronghold in a day of trouble.
You will protect him
if he takes refuge in you.
Nahum 1:7

65

Future

Reveal to

____

that there is
still a vision
for her appointed time.
If it seems like it tarries,
that she should wait for it,
because it will surely come,
and it will not delay.
Habakkuk 2:3

66

FUTURE PLENTY

Help

---

understand that
anyone who tills the land
will have plenty of bread.
But one who follows
worthless pursuits
will have plenty of poverty.
Proverbs 28:19

67

PROTECTION

Keep

____

as the apple of your eye;
hide him in the
shadow of your wings
from the wicked
who assail him,
from mortal enemies
who surround him.
Psalm 17:8-9

68

Destiny

Fulfill your
purpose for

______________________;

do not abandon
the works of your hands.
Psalm 138:8

69

Comings and Goings

Watch over
______________'s

life.
Do not slumber or sleep,
but keep her from all harm.
Watch over her life,
her coming and going,
both now and forevermore.
Psalm 121:3-8

70

APPOINTMENT

Give

______________________,

a sense of destiny,
and show her
that you set her apart
and appointed her
with gifts
and talents
even before
she was born.
Jeremiah 1:5

71

Plans to Prosper

You know the plans
you have for

_______________________,

plans to prosper him
and not to harm him,
plans to give him hope
and a future.
Cause

____

to call upon you
and come and pray to you,
and then listen to him,
O Lord.
Let him seek you
with all his heart,
and find you
when he does seek you.
Jeremiah 29:11

72

FRIENDS WHO HELP

Bless

____

with friends,
and let him
be a friend
to the friendless,
since "two are better than one...
If one falls down,
his friend can help him up.
But pity the man
who falls
and has no one
to help him up!"
Ecclesiastes 4:9-10

73

Friends who Love

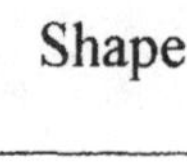

into a friend
who loves
at all times.
Proverbs 17:17

74

Friends who Sharpen

Surround

____

with friends
who will sharpen her
as iron
sharpens iron.
Proverbs 27:17

75

Patience

Thank you
that no eye has seen,
no ear has heard,
no mind has conceived
what you have
prepared for

____

because he loves you.
Cause him to be
willing to wait on you,
and act on his behalf.
1 Corinthians 2:9

76

BEGIN AND COMPLETE

Thank you
for beginning
a good work in

______________________,

and that you
will carry it on
to completion
until the day
of Christ Jesus.
Philippians 1:6

77

Future

Thank you
for loving

---

so much that you gave
your one and only Son,
that when

---

believes in him,
she will not perish
but have eternal life.
John 3:16

78

FORGET THE PAST

Don't let

---

be burdened
by her past.
Remind her that
if anyone is
in Christ,
she is
a new creation;
2 Corinthians 5:17

79

Fulfilled Purpose

Fulfill every
good purpose in

____________________'s

life
and every act
prompted by her faith,
so that the name
of our Lord Jesus Christ
may be glorified in her life.
2 Thessalonians 1:11-12

80

YOUR PURPOSE

No matter what

____

is planning in his heart,
let your purpose
prevail in his life.
Proverbs 19:21

TIMEOUT REFLECTIONS ON DANIELLE

ELEMENTARY SCHOOL STUDENT PROFILE

REFLECT ON DANIELLE

Danielle was a special child. She was the oldest girl and second child in the house. She had two younger sisters with apparent stronger academic capabilities than her. She was the big sister, but not the smartest sister. In fact, both she and her brother demonstrated intellectual challenges. Her mother was not married and had never been married to any of her four children's fathers.

Danielle grew up in a single parent home and experienced all the symptoms of children where their mother incorporated different men in their home for short periods of time. She witnessed her mother's physical abuse, emotional abuse, substance abuse, evictions, state aid, little to no medical treatment, and little to rare involvement with her own father. Her brother's father was in prison. Most of the school year, Danielle's sisters lived with their father.

Danielle never learned phonics and struggled to repeat words as she thought she heard them. In fact, Danielle could repeat the conversations word for word from every person she met, but could not read first grade basic sight words. Danielle was in the sixth grade and she could not count, write or spell. Although she failed the second grade, her teachers moved her on each year to the next grade level.

Yet Danielle had a sweet disposition. She was helpful and quite affectionate. She could dance and she loved to sing. She also understood that she didn't know as much as her classmates or her younger sisters.

Danielle started facing some major challenges in school and her mother declared herself to be the best parent alive. Danielle's mother did not offer more assistance because she could not, and either blamed Danielle's mental challenges on her father or the school. Danielle's mother had little to no academic skills herself, so tutoring wasn't received. The school encouraged her to place Danielle into the Special Education program.

Danielle's mother seemed pleased that Danielle was now part of the thousands of children that receive instruction deemed for students who have academic or mental challenges. However, her mother didn't grasp that Danielle still couldn't spell first grade words, pronounce or write the name of her new street or count change at the store accurately.

RESPOND

Chapter Five
Guidance~Choices

Read Prayers of Intercession

81

Direction

Guide

to have the power
to comprehend,
what is the breadth
and length and height and depth,
and your love
that surpasses knowledge,
so that he may be filled
with all the fullness of God.
Ephesians 3:18-20

82

LIGHTED PATHWAY

Direct

so that she will
embrace your word
as a lamp to her feet
and a light
for her path.
Psalm 119:105

83

PROMISES

Show

____________________,

that your way
is perfect
and your promises
prove true.
Be her shield
as she takes
refuge in you.
2 Samuel 22:31

84

Counsel

Counsel and guide

Lord.
Instruct him,
even
during the night.
Psalm 16:7

85

Right and Wrong

Give

---

a wise
and discerning heart
so that she
can distinguish
between right
and wrong.
1 Kings 3:9,12

86

Positive Choices

Bless and keep

________________________,

so that she
will not walk
in the counsel
of the wicked
or stand in the way
of sinners
or sit in the seat
of mockers.
Psalm 1:1

87

ASSAULTED

When

____

is set upon by bullies
or assaulted
by other wickedness,
please help him
and deliver him.
Deliver him
from the wicked
and save him,
because he takes
refuge in you.
Psalm 37:40

88

SECURITY

I pray that

____

would put
her trust in you
and never
be shaken.
Psalm 125:1

89

Shield

Hem

---

in behind and before;
place your hand
upon her
so that
wherever she goes
and whatever she does,
she will be accompanied
by your presence.
Psalm 139:5-10

90

Net of Safety

Keep

____

from the snares
the enemy has laid for him,
from the traps
set by evildoers.
Let the wicked
fall into their own nets,
while he passes by in safety.
Psalm 141: 9-10

91

BE A GUARD

Give

____

victory and
be her shield.
Guard her course
and protect her way.
Proverbs 2:7-8

92

Unwise Friends

I pray that

____

would choose
his friends carefully,
for the way
of the wicked
leads them astray.
Proverbs 12:26

93

Evil Influences

Do not let

____

be led astray
by drugs
and alcohol.
Proverbs 20:1

94

TROUBLES IN LIFE

Lord, you have
summoned

____

by name
and he belongs to you.
When he passes
through the waters,
be with him;
when he passes through the rivers,
do not let them
sweep him away.
When he walks
through the fire,
do not let him be burned.
And when

____

emerges from these trials,
let him know
that you are his God,
that you are
the Holy One of Israel,
and that you are his Savior.

95

Everlasting Covenant

Give

____

one heart and one way,
and be her God.
so that she may
fear you for all time,
for her own good.
Make an everlasting
covenant with

___________________.

Never stop doing
good to her,
and inspire her to fear you
so that she will
never turn away
from you.
Jeremiah 32:39-40

96

TEMPTATION

Lead

---

not into temptation,
but deliver her
from the evil one.
Matthew 6:13

97

SPIRIT DIRECTED

Let

____

live by the Spirit
and be
guided by the Spirit.
Let

____

not become
conceited competing against
another or envying another.
Galatians 5:25-26

98

APPRECIATION

Remind

---

to pray
for his teachers
and coaches
and give thanks
for the role
they play in his life.
1 Timothy 2:1-2

99

CHOOSE GOD

Let

____

seek friendship
with you rather
than with the world,
remembering that anyone
who chooses to be a friend
of the world
becomes your enemy.
James 4:4

100

MISLEADING FRIENDS

Do not let
anyone lead

____

astray.
Cause him to do
what is righteous
rather than what is sinful.
Thank you for sending
your Son
to destroy
the devil's work.
1 John 3:7-8

Timeout Reflections on Keith

High School Student Profile

Reflect on Keith

Keith was a tremendous athlete. Every team sport he participated in gave him opportunity to showcase his athletic skills and talents. He was popular with the students and all his coaches loved him. But Keith carried a lot of personal and home baggage, and the load didn't seem to ease. Keith couldn't cut the grade with his academic courses. All of his teachers reported his failure to complete assignments, his laise-faire attitude and his high absenteeism.

In his senior year, Keith found himself on the Team Sports Ineligible Players List. For every team sport, he faced some hurdles and the team faced the eight ball. The coaches had their backs against the wall. He was their MVP, but he was failing all of his academic courses. During football, basketball land baseball season, he faithfully practiced every evening. He was never late for a game or practice. He worked hard earning his starting positions. But for every first game, the coaches panicked about his eligibility. Keith went around with his coaches seeking mercy from the teachers.

Issues of integrity surfaced regarding slipping him into the game. Questions were raised about changing his failing grades. Commitment, dedication and sacrifice were debated regarding academic achievement, faithfulness, personal and team responsibility and maturity.

Many standards and expectations were broken, adjusted and reappropriated on Keith's behalf. This pattern repeated itself over and over. Yet young Keith didn't demonstrate appreciation. He took it in stride as an expected perk for his talent. Keith never re-enrolled in any of his failing courses. Many skills were not acquired in necessary subjects. Keith missed several opportunities to appreciate day by day classroom instruction. Keith sent no thank you cards to the teachers or administration. No tears rolled down his cheeks at the graduation ceremony.

Keith became another statistic that left high school unprepared to face the classrooms of higher learning, but sufficiently prepared to score a touchdown, make a two-point basket, and hit a homerun.

His focus was singular in effort. His ethical and moral development, his sense of right and wrong, and his yearning for favoritism were misaligned. He saw by example that pulling strings was the name of the current game he learned to excel.

The death of his single parent at an early age no doubt caused trauma and layers of pain, and he never knew his father. So he became a survivor.

Respond

CHAPTER SIX
TEACHABLE SPIRITS

READ PRAYERS OF INTERCESSION

101

New Heart ~ New Spirit

Provide

____

with a new heart
and put
a new spirit
within him.
Remove his heart
of stone
and give him
a heart of flesh.
so that

____

may follow your statues
and keep your ordinances.
Ezekiel 11:19-20

102

Pleasantness

Teach

____

to do all things
without murmuring
and arguing,
so that she may
be blameless and innocent,
without blemish
in the midst of
a crooked and
perverse generation,
in which she may shine
like stars in this world.
Philippians 2:14

103

Openness

Permit

____

to listen and
be open to advice
and accept instruction,
that she may gain
wisdom for the future.
Proverbs 19:20

104

Agreeable

Present to

____

that he be agreeable
and cause no
disagreements among others.
Help him understand
he should be united
with the same mind
and for the same purpose.
1 Corinthians 1:10

105

Warnings

Teach

____

to keep his life free
from the love of money,
and to be content
with what he has.
For you have shared
that you will never leave

____

or forsake him.
Hebrews 13:5

106

BEST BUYS

Show

---

that she should
buy truth
and not sell it.
Reveal to her that
she should
buy wisdom,
instruction and
understanding.
Proverbs 23:23

107

Rooted

Allow

____________________,

to be rooted
and built up
in Christ Jesus,
and established in faith
just as he was taught,
and abounding
in thanksgiving.
Colossians 2:7

108

IMITATOR

Let

________________________,

be an
imitator of
Christ Jesus.
1 Corinthians 11:1

109

Insight

Make
___________________'s

ear attentive to wisdom
and incline her heart
to understanding.
Give her a teachable spirit,
one that cries out for insight.
Proverbs 2:2-3

110

Instruction

Teach

______________________,

not to make friends
with those given to anger.
Do not let him
associate with hotheads
so that he
will not learn their ways
and entangle himself in a snare.
Proverbs 22:24-25

111

PARENTAL RESPECT

Thank you for

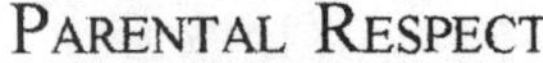.

Teach him
to listen to his father
who birthed him,
and not
to despise his mother
when she is old.
Proverbs 23:22

112

NEW HEART

Give

____

a new heart
and put a new spirit
within

____________________.

Remove his
heart of stone
and give him
a heart of flesh.
Ezekiel 11:19

113

Favor

Let all who hear

---

be amazed
at his understanding
and his answers.
And let his parents
be astonished
at his favor from you
Oh, God.
Luke 2:47-48

114

Fruitful Soil

Allow
_________________'s

spirit to be
like good soil,
so when
he hears your word,
he will hold it fast
in an honest
and good heart,
and bear fruit
with patient endurance.
Luke 8:15

115

Emotions

Show

---

that you have
set us free
from the emotional
traps of this world,
and encourage

---

to stand firm
and never to submit again
to any emotional
yoke of slavery.
Galatians 5:1

116

Submission To Authority

Permit

____

to understand
that he should
obey all his leaders
and teachers
and submit to us.
Help him accept
that we are keeping watch
over his soul and
that we too
will give an account
to you how we
interact with him.
Hebrews 13:17

117

GOOD BEHAVIOR

Help

---

understand that
she should
avoid stupid controversies,
dissentions and quarrels
for it is unprofitable
and worthless to her growth.
Titus 3:9

118

BE A DOER AND HEARER

Teach

____

to be a
doer of the word,
and not merely
a hearer
who deceives
himself.
James 1:22

119

GRACEFUL SELF-CONTROL

Prepare
________________________'s

mind for action.
Teach her
to discipline herself,
and set her hope
on the grace
that Jesus Christ
will bring when
you are revealed.
1 Peter 1:13

120

Choose Good

Raise up

---

so that he
does not imitate
what is evil,
but imitates
what is good.
Whoever does good
is from God,
Whoever does evil
has not seen God.
3 John 11

Timeout Reflections With Marcus

Middle School Student Profile

REFLECT ON MARCUS

The start of the semester proved to be life changing for Marcus. He was in the eighth grade and made friends with some older boys in the neighborhood. Although he seemed a little more grounded than the year before, his quiet demeanor still hovered around his persona. His eyes always revealed his willingness to take time and process. He was not one to shout out any comment. No, Marcus took time to consider his response before sharing. Frequently, his Social Studies classmates would inquire how he knew a particular answer about geographical or societal issues. Marcus would state his interest in research and investigation. Marcus was not overly aggressive or an attention seeker in class. He rarely got into arguments with the other boys. But he was no angel, nor did he seem intimidated. In fact, he always had a semi plastered half-open smile on his face. He had a Dennis the Menace look about him.

Yet no one knew what forced his smile. None of his teachers thought much about this teenager except to know him by face and not by any extraordinary skills or talents. He was just an average student with potential to demonstrate more with encouragement.

But something happened in October. Unknown to most of the students and teachers, Marcus had a dark side. He started skipping school. Sometimes he would come to school in the middle of the day without a parent or note. His attention seemed to be minimal and he stopped contributing to the class discussions like before.

Then just before Thanksgiving, Marcus became engaged in some non-typical behaviors. He started fighting in school. When Marcus returned from the holiday break he reported that his mother had died. This of course was traumatic, and his classmates showed compassion. The principal and several staff went to the funeral, where Marcus read a poem about his feelings for his mother. He didn't shed a tear. It seemed quite a sad day, but he returned to school the next day as if nothing happened.

However, as police continued investigations, news raced to the school and community that Marcus had a tragic part in his mother's death. It was reported that Marcus set up a plan for his mother's demise with one of the older neighborhood boys. A silent witness overheard the quarrel from the basement and informed the police about Marcus' part. No one knew about the witness. Certainly, not Marcus, nor the neighborhood friend. And no one really knew Marcus. Not his classmates, or his teachers or his family. Young Marcus was arrested, and his life will never be the same.

RESPOND

CHAPTER SEVEN
WISDOM AND KNOWLEDGE

Read Prayers of Intercession

121

AVOID EVIL

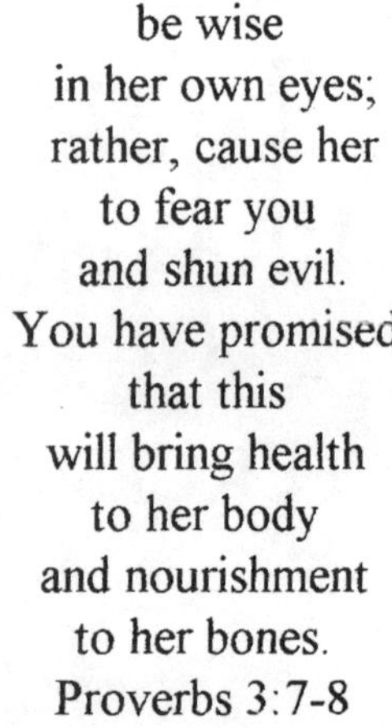

Don't let

____

be wise
in her own eyes;
rather, cause her
to fear you
and shun evil.
You have promised
that this
will bring health
to her body
and nourishment
to her bones.
Proverbs 3:7-8

122

Pursuit of Riches

Help

---

understand that
"he who gathers money
little by little
makes it grow."
Don't let

---

wear herself out
to get rich;
give her wisdom
she needs
to show restraint.
Proverbs 13:11; 23:4

123

VIRTUOUS WALK

Cause

to look carefully
how she walks,
not as unwise
but as wise,
making the most
of her time
and understanding
your will.
Ephesians 5:15

124

Turn from Evil

Open
______________'s

eyes so that
he may turn
from darkness
to light,
and from
the power of Satan
to you, O God,
so that he may receive
forgiveness of sins
and a place
among those
in Christ.
Acts 26:18

125

Faithful Over Gifts

Show

---

how to use
her gifts
and talents wisely,
being faithful
with the abilities
you have given her.
Matthew 25:21

126

COMMITMENT

Let

____

understand that
whatever her task,
she should put herself into it,
as done for you Lord,
and not for people.
Colossians 3:23

127

Careful Living

Let

____

be careful and wise
in how he lives,
making the most
of every opportunity
and understanding
your will for his life.
Ephesians 5:17

128

BLINDERS

Remove the
blinders from
_____________________'s

eyes, so that
he can be given
the light
of knowledge
of your glory
in the face
of Christ.
2 Corinthians 4:6

129

Persecution

May

---

realize that he
must love his enemies
and pray for those
who persecute him,
so that he may
be a child of the
Father in Heaven.
Matthew 5:44-45

130

Gift of Wisdom

Give

____

wisdom and
understanding.
Do not let
him forget your words.
Allow him to love wisdom
and to value and treasure it
above all worldly desires
and accomplishments.
Proverbs 4:5-7

131

Pathway of Life

Make known to

____

the path of life
and fill him
with joy
in your presence.
Psalm 16:7,11

132

Pressures of the World

Do not remove

____

from the pressures
and trials of this world,
but protect her from the evil one.
Remind her that
she belongs to you,
not to the world.
John 17:14-15

133

A Sure Answer

I pray that

____

would always be prepared
to give an answer
to everyone who asks her
to give the reason
for the hope that she has,
and cause her to speak
with gentleness and respect.
1 Peter 3:15

134

STOP CHEATING

Fill

---

with the knowledge
that he shall not
cheat another one,
but he shall
fear you God,
for you are the
Lord our God.
Leviticus 25: 17

135

God's Family

Let

____

know that
she belongs
to you
and she
is part
of your family.
Romans 14:7-9

136

Valuable Teachings

Let

______________________,

keep your commandments
and live.
Cause

____

to guard your teachings
as the apple of his eye,
and bind them
on his fingers
so that he
may write them
on the tablet
of his heart.
Proverbs 7:2-3

137

IDENTITY ASSURANCE

I pray that
_________________'s

identity
will be firmly
rooted and established
in Christ's love.
Ephesians 3:17

138

FULLNESS OF GOD

Bless

____

to have power,
together with all the saints,
to grasp how wide and long
and high and deep
is the love of Christ,
and to know this love
that surpasses knowledge-
that she may be filled
to the measure
of all the fullness
of God.
Ephesians 3:19

139

Inner Strength

According to the riches
of your glory
grant that

____________________,

be strengthened
in your inner being
with power
through your Spirit.
Ephesians 3:18

140

TRAINING IN RIGHTEOUSNESS

Show

______________________,

that all Scripture
is inspired by God
and is useful
for teaching,
for reproof,
for correction,
and for training
in righteousness.
2 Timothy 3:16

141

EYES OF GOD

Do not let

---

look at things
man looks at,
but let her see
the world
through your eyes
and respond to it
with your wisdom
and your love.
1 Samuel 16:7

142

WORTHY LIFE

Fill

______________________,

with the knowledge
of your will
through all spiritual wisdom
and understanding,
that he might live
a life worthy of you, Lord,
and please you
in every way.
Colossians 1:9-10

143

WISDOM

Your word says
that any one of us
who lack in wisdom,
should ask you
who gives to all
generously
and ungrudgingly.

Give

______________________,

wisdom.
James 1:5

144

WISE COUNSEL

Let your Spirit
rest on

____

Give him
the Spirit of wisdom
and understanding,
the Spirit of counsel
and power,
the Spirit of knowledge
and of the fear of the Lord-
that he might delight
in the fear of the Lord.
Don't let

____

judge by what he sees
with his eyes,
or decide by what he hears
with his ears,
but let him act
with righteousness,
justice and faith.
Isaiah 11:2-5

145

Worry

Allow

____

to not worry
and lie down
and
sleep in peace
and safety.
Psalm 4:8

146

Escape

Cause

---

to come
to know the truth
and escape
from the snare
of the devil,
who has
been held captive
to do his will.
2 Timothy 2:26

Timeout Reflections on Amy

University Student Profile

Reflect on Amy

Life on campus was going to be an eye-opening awakening for Amy. This was the first time, she ever stayed anywhere out of town without her parents. She was eighteen and she didn't go on dates in high school and she didn't even go to the prom. Needless to say, Amy had led a sheltered life, although not an innocent life. She found ways to experience many activities during the school hours.

She was the first one to go to college in her immediate family. Both her parents thought hard work provided a good quality of life. Her father believed the sooner she worked, the sooner he didn't have to pay for her things. Her father had talked about giving her time to find a job because she didn't seem to have any ambition or clear thoughts of a future career. But Amy applied to college as a way out of the house. She had quite enough of the house rules.

Amy's family didn't take her serious about attending college. It just wasn't respected in her home as valuable. And for that matter, neither did Amy. Amy wanted to let loose at her parent's expense. She already met some urban kids on the first day at orientation. She saw a couple of girls moving in and wondered if they had friends from another culture. Maybe this would be the first friendship for both. Amy seemed willing to try and offered to help. Amy thought they might know some male students on one of the teams. She hoped so. She wanted to be included.

After her first week away at school, she quickly became quite popular. Amy availed herself for every social mixer, party or activity that she could. She met people easily, and made arrangements to get class notes whenever possible.

Amy had made a plan, and she was working the plan. She called home often, but her roommates found her rarely in the dorm room. She didn't frequent the library, nor did she participate in study groups. She started missing lectures and started turning in her papers late. But she couldn't see a pattern developing. Everything was exciting and fun. School and studies were secondary at best. She just wanted to experience the college life.

Amy figured her parents didn't expect much anyway, and both her and her parents agreed she had four years to determine her life choice.

RESPOND

Chapter Eight
Trust in God

Read Prayers of Intercession

147

GUARDIAN ANGEL

Let

____

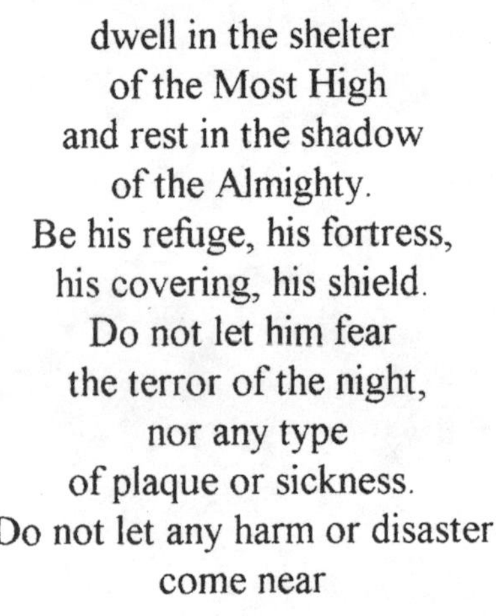

dwell in the shelter
of the Most High
and rest in the shadow
of the Almighty.
Be his refuge, his fortress,
his covering, his shield.
Do not let him fear
the terror of the night,
nor any type
of plaque or sickness.
Do not let any harm or disaster
come near

____

Command your angels
to guard him in all his ways
and keep him from hurting himself.
When he calls on you,
answer him. Be with him
in trouble;
deliver him and honor him.
Satisfy———— with long life
and show him your salvation.
Psalm 91

148

FENCE OF PROTECTION

Put a fence
around

____

and his house
and all that he has.
Job 1:10

149

BAD TEMPER

Show

____

that she should
not be angry
with her brother or sister,
or she will be liable to judgement.
Do not let her insult
her classmates or she will be
liable to administration.
Let her trust you
to work out the issue.
Matthew 5:22

150

SELF-RELIANCE

Encourage

____

to trust you
O Lord
with all his heart,
and do not rely
on his own insight.
Teach him
to acknowledge you
in all his ways
and you will
make straight his paths.
Proverbs 3:5-6

151

Arrogance

Don't let

____

become haughty or
set his hopes
on the uncertainty of riches,
but let him put
his trust in you
who richly provides us
with everything for our enjoyment.
Teach him to do good,
be generous and ready to share.
1 Timothy 6:17-18

152

MISLEADING TEACHERS

Don't let any
teacher take

____

captive through philosophy,
and empty deceit
according to
human tradition,
and the basic elements
of this universe,
and not according to
faith in Christ.
Colossians 2:8

153

PATIENT TEACHERS

Teach
______________________’s

teachers
not to grow weary
in doing and teaching
what is right,
but let us know
we will reap at harvest
if we do not give up.
Galatians 6:9

154

HANDPICKED TEACHERS

Reveal to

____

that all things work
together for good,
for those who love God.
Allow him to trust
that he has teachers
who are called
according to God's purpose.
Romans 8:28

155

CARING TEACHERS

Show me
as a teacher
how to tend
to your flock
like a shepherd.
Show me how
to gently lead and care
for your students
especially
____________________,
like a mother sheep.
Isaiah 40:11

156

FULL ARMOR OF PROTECTION

Allow

____

to put on
the whole armor of God,
so that he
may be able to stand
against the wiles of the devil.
Show him that
his struggle is not
against enemies of blood and flesh,
but against the rulers,
against the authorities,
against the cosmic powers
of this present darkness,
against the spiritual forces of evil
in the heavenly places.
Ephesians 6:11-18

157

Careful Words

Comfort

_________________,

so that he knows
wherever he goes,
you will be his mouth
and teach him
what he is to speak.
Exodus 4:12

158

Grateful Heart

Give

____

an understanding
and grateful heart that
God is faithful
and he will strengthen her
and guard her
from wicked and evil people.
2 Thessalonians 3:3

159

Riches From God

Reveal to

____

Oh God,
that you
will fully satisfy
every need of his
according to your riches
in glory in Christ Jesus.
Philippians 4:19

160

APPROVAL

Help

---

do things with
gentleness and reverence.
Keep her conscience clear,
so that,
when she is maligned,
those who abuse her
for her good conduct
in Christ
may be put to shame.
1 Peter 3:16

161

Unkind Words

Show

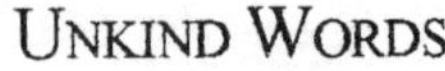

how to
take shelter
in your presence
to hide her
from human
plots and tricks.
Keep her safe
under your shelter
from contentious tongues.
Psalm 31:20

162

STRONGHOLDS

Prepare
_______________'s

heart to know
that the weapons
of our warfare
are not merely human,
but they have
divine power
to destroy strongholds.
Reveal to her
that she may
destroy arguments
and every proud obstacle
raised up against her
through the knowledge of God.
2 Corinthians 10: 4-5

163

RESIST TEMPTATIONS

Help

____

to submit himself
to you.
O God,
and to resist the devil,
so the devil
will flee from

____________________.

James 4:7

164

UNCERTAINTY

Teach

____

not to fear,
for you are with her.
Show

____

you will strengthen her
and help her,
and that you
will uphold her
with your victorious
right hand.
Isaiah 41:0

165

Firm in Faith

Keep

---

alert,
standing firm
in his faith,
being courageous
and strong.
1Corinthians 16:13

166

PAST HISTORY CONFESSION

Let

____

trust you
to believe
that if he is in Christ,
there is a new creation,
everything old has passed away
and everything has become new.
2 Cor. 5:17

Timeout Reflections on Anastacia

Private School Student Profile

REFLECT ON ANASTACIA

Anastacia led an international life from birth. She was born in London, annexed to wealth. Her father was a French doctor and her mother was an Caribbean lawyer. Yet Anastacia never lived the life of luxury because her parents were never married. Her father's French culture and family dictated that she be exempted or withheld appropriate nurturing because of her mother's Caribbean heritage. Although her parents' co-habitation survived the British traditions, when her father moved back to Paris to continue his practice, he immediately dismissed her mother and all claims to Anastacia. Anastacia and her mother were forced to return to the Caribbean and temporarily live on the support of her mother's family.

Trauma and identity started very early in her life. Her mother was determined to keep Anastacia's educational experience with the top private schools money could afford. Her mother's legal experience victoriously culminated in Anastacia's education continuing with America's elite. But Anastacia grew up in confusion, rumors, prejudice and several country's racial intolerance. She was always forced to defend one parent to another. She hated her skin, her long hair and sometimes her mother.

She demonstrated academic achievement, but she felt insecure, and genuinely unloved. She was denied by her paternal grandparents and often left to live with a host family in America, when her mother's traveling visa was not honored. She looked pretty on the outside by all standards, but felt ugly and pain inwardly. She couldn't wait to grow up. She wouldn't make the same mistake her mother made. She would be smarter than her mother. She planned to study medicine like her father, and embrace the things her grandparents denied her.

But then one day, her mother sent for her to return to the islands. She hadn't seen her mother for almost a year. When she arrived in the islands, her mother was carrying a baby.

Anastacia had a new sister, and she looked like Anastacia. Tears flowed down her cheeks as she reflected her earlier years. Anastacia was sixteen, but she cried like she was six.

RESPOND